Non-Religio

Poetry and Prose for Civil Marriage Ceremonies

Compiled by Hugh Morrison

Montpelier Publishing
London
MMXIV

Published by Montpelier Publishing, London.
Printed by Amazon Createspace.
Set in Calibri 11pt.

Somewhere

Somewhere there waiteth in this world of ours
For one lone soul, another lonely soul—
Each chasing each through all the weary hours,
And meeting strangely at one sudden goal;
Then blend they—like green leaves with golden flowers,
Into one beautiful and perfect whole—
And life's long night is ended, and the way
Lies open onward to eternal day.

Sir Edwin Arnold (1832-1904)

Tell each other daily of your love

After marriage do not forget to speak the gentle words you used to say; repeat those kindnesses. Tell each other daily of your love. We never weary of these words, 'I love, I love.' These are the sweetest sounds the ear has ever heard, and always fresh and new.

Do not take for granted that your wife knows you love her, but often tell her so. She is never so old and grey, but that to tell her you love her as in her earlier day, will add youth to looks and lightness to her step.

No man so far advanced in years, but for his wife to gently smooth his hair, and tell him of her love, will add lustre to his eye, and strength to limb.

Make little presents now and then, not rich expensive gifts that one could ill afford; not costly jewels, expensive ornaments, nor things quite out of reach. It is the little kindnesses which make love more sweet.

Anna M. Longshore-Potts (1829-1912)

Love is not a summer mood

Oh, love is not a summer mood,
Nor flying phantom of the brain,
Nor youthful fever of the blood.

Nor dream, nor fate, nor circumstance.
Love is not born of blinded chance.
Nor bred in simple ignorance.

Love is the flower of maidenhood;
Love is the fruit of mortal pain;
And she hath winter in her blood.

True love is steadfast as the skies,
And once alight she never flies;
And love is strong, and love is wise.

Richard Watson Gilder (1844-1909)

Life is ever born anew

Inorganic matter, stones, earth, mountains, hills, the sea, remain as they were; they endure for hundreds of thousands of years. But life, which in human form expresses itself in terms of thinking, feeling, and willing, is ever born anew, and would perish utterly were it not renewed.

Marriage is an institution for saving life, the best thing in the world, for saving the most delicate and precious thing, mentality; and not only for saving it, but for improving and refining it with every renewal.

At all events, the great current of evolution sweeps through us; and the thing in all this universe of suns and stars that is most worth preserving, increasing, and enhancing life, this it is which renews itself through husband and wife.

Felix Adler (1851-1933)

Because she would ask me why I loved her

If questioning would make us wise
No eyes would ever gaze in eyes;

If all our tale were told in speech
No mouths would wander each to each.

Were spirits free from mortal mesh
And love not bound in hearts of flesh

No aching breasts would yearn to meet
And find their ecstasy complete.

For who is there that lives and knows
The secret powers by which he grows?

Were knowledge all, what were our need
To thrill and faint and sweetly bleed?

Then seek not, sweet, the 'If' and 'Why'
I love you now until I die.

For I must love because I live
And life in me is what you give.

Christopher Brennan (1870-1932)

Take here my heart, I give it thee for ever!

Take here my heart, I give it thee for ever!
No better pledge can love to love deliver.
Fear not, my dear, it will not fly away
For hope and love command my heart to stay.
But if thou doubt, desire will make it range:
Love but my heart, my heart will never change.

Thomas Weelkes (1576-1623)

The power of great love

Even at the present day couples are to be found who are inspired by great love. They show an insatiable desire for all the riches of life, so as to have the means of being regally lavish towards each other. Neither defrauds the other of so much as a dewdrop. The fervour they give one another, the freedom they possess through one another, make the space that surrounds them warm and ample.

Love is constantly giving them new impulses, new powers and new employment for their powers, whether these are directed inwards to home life or outwards to that of society. And thus the happiness, which for themselves is the source of life, becomes also a tributary stream by which the happiness of all is raised. The power of great love to enhance a person's value for mankind can only be compared with the glow of religious faith or the creative joy of genius, but surpasses both in universal life-enhancing properties.

Sorrow may sometimes make a person more tender towards the sufferings of others, more actively benevolent than happiness with its concentration upon self. But sorrow never led the soul to those heights and depths, to those inspirations and revelations of universal life, to that kneeling gratitude before the mystery of life, to which the piety of great love leads it.

Like faith, this piety sanctifies all things.

Ellen Key (1849-1926)

Hearts with equal love combined

He that loves a rosy cheek,
Or a coral lip admires,
Or from star-like eyes doth seek
Fuel to maintain his fires;
As old Time makes these decay,
So his flames must waste away.
But a smooth and steadfast mind,
Gentle thoughts and calm desires,
Hearts with equal love combined,
Kindle never-dying fires;
Where these are not, I despise
Lovely cheeks, or lips, or eyes.

Thomas Carew (1595-1640)

Something infinitely more

I have often said that marriage seems to me to be the epitome of all other fine relations. There is a certain element of brotherliness in it as between the married pair; there is a certain fatherly attitude; there is a certain motherly brooding on the part of the wife over her husband; there is friendship, and an element of comradeship; and there is always something infinitely more.

What is that something infinitely more? It is something present in no other human relation. It is just the feeling that, as between husband and wife, there shall be a total blending of mind with mind and heart with heart; that they shall touch not merely at one point, as friends or companions do, but that they shall touch at all points; that they cannot endure separation....true husband and wife cannot live one on this side of the water and the other on the other side.

They are moved to have all things in common, to live under the same roof, to break bread together day by day, to pass through the vicissitudes of life together, to suffer with each other, to rejoice together, to learn life's lessons together; to wish to confer perpetual benefit each on the other.

They are not romantic enthusiasts, neither are they without the poetic rapture in each other's relation. The true love of marriage differs from romantic love in this, that the romantic lover sees perfection contrary to the facts, and attributes a present perfection to the other; the real lover is he who sees a certain excellence, a certain charm without the attraction of that there would be no approach but beyond that, sees the possibility of greater excellence and perfection which is not yet, but which shall be developed through mutual help.

Felix Adler (1851-1933)

Not ours the vows

Not ours the vows of such as plight
Their troth in sunny weather,
While leaves are green and skies are bright,
To walk on flowers together.

But we have loved as those who tread
The thorny path of sorrow,
With clouds above, and cause to dread
Yet deeper gloom to-morrow.

That thorny path, those stormy skies,
Have drawn our spirits nearer;
And rendered us, by sorrow's ties,
Each to the other dearer.

Love, born in hours of joy and mirth,
With mirth and joy may perish;
That to which darker hours gave birth
Still more and more we cherish.

It looks beyond the clouds of time,
And through death's shadowy portal;
Made by adversity sublime,
By faith and hope immortal.

Bernard Barton (1784-1849)

Aim to be happy every day

If therefore married persons expect to love one another throughout life, however long the journey may be, they must study to make themselves worthy of one another's love. We cannot love what is unlovely.

Happiness will not come to us unless we pursue the proper method of obtaining it. Some there are who tell us that 'the pleasure of expecting enjoyment is often greater than that of obtaining it, and that the completion of almost every wish is found a disappointment.'

If this be true, then determine to be happy. You must expect to meet with many things to interrupt your quiet enjoyment of life. Never mind; look at the bright side of things; or, as the old saying has it, 'never cross a bridge until you come to it.' Aim to be happy every day.

John William Kirton (1831-1892)

The fire of love

The fire of love in youthful blood,
Like what is kindled in brushwood,
But for a moment burns;
Yet in that moment makes a mighty noise;
It crackles, and to vapour turns,
And soon itself destroys.
But when crept into agèd veins
It slowly burns, and then long remains,
And with a silent heat,
Like fire in logs, it glows and warms them long,
And though the name be not so great,
Yet is the heat as strong.

Charles Sackville, Earl of Dorset (1638-1706)

The brightness of joy

One of the secrets of making home-life happy, is the rare faculty of looking habitually on the sunny side of things—of wearing ever a cheerful smile. This will dissipate the darkness of sorrow, and irradiate the brightness of joy—will disarm the former of its sting, and impart a zest to the latter that nothing else can supply.

A cheerful, quiet spirit, that finds its truest enjoyment in accepting life as it is,—determined to make the best of it,—is a boon whose value is above rubies. A spirit that indulges not in scandal, but draws the mantle of charity over all faults and frailties, and notes only the bright features of charity:—such a temper of mind sheds a halo of beauty over the face, also, that even old age cannot destroy.

Frederick Saunders (1807-1902)

Live to love

Love is life's end! An end but never ending;
All joy, all sweets, all happiness awarding,
Loves is life's wealth (ne'er spent, but ever spending),
More rich by giving, taking by discarding,
Love's life's reward, rewarded in rewarding;
Then from they wretched heart fond care remove;
Ah! Should'st thou live but love's sweets to prove,
Thou wilt not love to live, unless thou live to love.

Sir Edmund Spenser (c.1552-1599)

Catch more flies with honey

Strive therefore to draw out each other's good qualities, and at the same time, if possible, to avoid arousing any of the evil ones.

Cultivate a desire to please, on the one hand, and a desire to be pleased on the other; then strife and contention will have but little chance of any existence.

You will 'catch more flies with honey than with vinegar,' says the old proverb. Try the experiment in daily life, and see how well it will work for good.

John William Kirton (1831-1892)

Hail wedded love

Hail wedded love, mysterious law, true source
Of human offspring, sole propriety,
In paradise of all things common else.
By thee adulterous lust was driven from men
Among the bestial herds to range, by thee
Founded in reason, loyal, just, and pure,
Relations dear, and all the charities
Of father, son, and brother first were known.
Far be it, that I should write thee sin or blame,
Of think thee unbefitting holiest place,
Perpetual fountain of domestic sweets,
Whose bed is undefiled and chaste pronounced,
Present, or past, as saints and patriarchs used.
Here love his golden shafts employs, here lights
His constant lamp, and waves his purple wings,
Reigns here and revels; not in the bought smile
Of harlots, loveless, joyless, unendeared,
Casual fruition, nor in court amours
Mixed dance, or wanton mask, or midnight ball,
Or serenade, which the starved lover sings
To his proud fair, best quitted with disdain.
These lulled by Nightingales embracing slept,
And on their naked limbs the flowery roof
Showered roses, which the morn repaired. Sleep on,
Blest pair; and O yet happiest if ye seek
No happier state, and know to know no more.

John Milton (1608-1674)

Love makes obedience lighter than liberty

The banes of domestic life are littleness, falsity, vulgarity, harshness, scolding vociferation, an incessant issuing of superfluous prohibitions and orders, which are regarded as impertinent interferences with general liberty and repose, and are provocative of rankling or exploding resentments.

The blessed antidotes that sweeten and enrich domestic life are refinement, high aims, great interests, soft voices, quiet and gentle manners, magnanimous tempers, forbearance from all unnecessary commands or dictation, and generous allowances of mutual freedom.

Love makes obedience lighter than liberty. Man wears a noble allegiance, not as a collar, but as a garland. The Graces are never so lovely as when seen waiting on the Virtues; and, where they thus dwell together, they make a heavenly home.

William Rounseville Alger (1822-1905)

True Love is a sacred flame

True Love is a sacred flame that burns eternally.
And none can dim its special glow or change its destiny.
True Love speaks in tender tones and hears with gentle ear.
True Love gives with open heart and True Love conquers fear.
True Love makes no harsh demands. It neither rules nor binds.
True Love holds with gentle hands the hearts that it entwines.

Anon

The woman who is loves and is beloved

The ideal wife, then, will sedulously cultivate the happy spirit of contentment, and make the best of everything, not seeking to add to the burden an already overworked husband may have to carry... The woman who loves and is beloved finds herself strong to bear the ills that may meet her from day to day.

The ideal husband, then, is no more perfect than the ideal wife; nor would she wish him to be other than he is, manly, generous, kindly-hearted, well-conditioned, and, above all things, true as steel.

It is well with the man who has in his wife not only a bright companion for his days of sunshine, but who in the crises of his life finds in her heart the jewel of common sense and the pearl of a quick understanding.

Annie Shepherd Swan (1859-1943)

Love has no other desire

Love has no other desire but to fulfill itself.
But if you love and must needs have desires, let these be your desires:
To melt and be like a running brook that sings its melody to the night.
To know the pain of too much tenderness.
To be wounded by your own understanding of love;
And to bleed willingly and joyfully.
To wake at dawn with a winged heart and give thanks for another day of loving;
To rest at the noon hour and meditate love's ecstasy;
To return home at eventide with gratitude;
And then to sleep with a prayer for the beloved in your heart and a song of praise on your lips.

Kahil Gilbran (1883-1931)

Marriage is the mother of the world

Marriage is a school and exercise of virtue; and though marriage hath cares, yet the single life hath desires which are more troublesome and more dangerous, and often end in sin, while the cares are but instances of duty and exercises of piety ; and, therefore, if single life hath more privacy of devotion, yet marriage hath more necessities and more variety of it, and is an exercise of more graces. Here kindness is spread abroad, and love is united and made firm as a centre.

Marriage is the mother of the world, and preserves kingdoms and fills cities and churches. Celibacy, like the fly in the heart of an apple, dwells in perpetual sweetness, but sits alone and is confined, and at last dies in singleness; but marriage, like the useful bee, builds a house and gathers sweetness from every flower—labours and unites into societies — sends out colonies and fills the world with delicacies.

It has its labours of love, its sweets of friendship, the blessings of society and the union of hands and hearts. It has in it less of beauty and more of safety than a single life. It is more merry and yet more sad; it is fuller of joys and yet fuller of sorrows. It lies under burdens, but it is supported by all the strength of love and charity, and these very burdens are delightful to be borne.

Jeremy Taylor (1613-1667)

The daily sweetness of this life with thee

The daily sweetness of this life with thee
And nightly wonder: these the sun and stars
Duly attest. Their risings and their settings
Are witness hourly to the light of thee
As of thy love, thy love lighting the world.
Thus as the sun and stars thy risings and
Thy lyings down are life unto the world,
Its motion and its impulse. In thy peace,
Passing all understanding of the spheres,
May earth or star or sun alike perform
Its perfect function. And within thy peace
I ponder of the life of sun and stars.

Reginald Chauncey Robbins (1871-1955)

Accept each other's faults

To the man or woman, however, who marries for that love which is based on the qualities of both head and heart, and who knows that daily life, with its rubs and scrubs, will sometimes mar the sweetest temper and cloud the serenest brow, there cannot come any serious disillusionment.

Loving each other dearly, they remember they are but human; and as perfection is not inborn in humanity, they accept each other's faults and shortcomings gracefully, not magnifying them sourly and grumblingly, but bearing with them, and rejoicing in and accepting the good.

Annie Shepherd Swan (1859-1943)

Unending love

I seem to have loved you in numberless forms, numberless times...
In life after life, in age after age, forever.
My spellbound heart has made and remade the necklace of songs,
That you take as a gift, wear round your neck in your many forms,
In life after life, in age after age, forever.

Whenever I hear old chronicles of love, its age-old pain,
Its ancient tale of being apart or together.
As I stare on and on into the past, in the end you emerge,
Clad in the light of a pole-star piercing the darkness of time:
You become an image of what is remembered forever.

You and I have floated here on the stream that brings from the
fount.
At the heart of time, love of one for another.
We have played along side millions of lovers, shared in the same
Shy sweetness of meeting, the same distressful tears of farewell—
Old love but in shapes that renew and renew forever.

Today it is heaped at your feet, it has found its end in you
The love of all man's days both past and forever:
Universal joy, universal sorrow, universal life.
The memories of all loves merging with this one love of ours –
And the songs of every poet past and forever.

Rabindranath Tagore (1861-1941)

A happy future

There can be no gentle manners, no true refinement, where selfishness is encouraged. Mere surface imitation there may be, but the lack of genuineness is readily perceived. All that really belongs to good manners must have its roots in unselfishness. It must spring up out of a spirit that really cares for others, and so will be genial and tender. Let selfishness grow, and there sometimes may be an outward deportment that passes for gentility, but it is a mere veneering that is speedily worn away...

The people who try to be generous, self-sacrificing, and self-denying may seem to be the losers, but look ahead, and see the difference between their home and the selfish home... Let each plan the other's happiness and be content to be self-restrained and patient, and ever ready for self-denial and sacrifices, and there is a happy future.

George Wolf Shinn (1839-1910)

Dear, if you change

Dear, if you change, I'll never choose again;
Sweet, if you shrink, I'll never think of love;
Fair, if you fail, I'll judge all beauty vain;
Wise, if too weak, more wits I'll never prove.
Dear, sweet, fair, wise! change, shrink, nor be not weak;
And, on my faith, my faith shall never break.
Earth with her flowers shall sooner heaven adorn;
Heaven her bright stars through earth's dim globe shall move;
Fire heat shall lose, and frosts of flames be born;
Air, made to shine, as black as hell shall prove:
Earth, heaven, fire, air, the world transformed shall view,
Ere I prove false to faith or strange to you.

John Dowland (1563-1626)

The fire in the heart

The fire in the heart must be fed by fuel proper for it, and where two people faithfully try to keep the flame burning the fuel is always at hand.

The wife may lose the charm of her youth, but her soul may grow more beautiful with advancing years. The husband may become broken with age, but his character may take on it, for her, a new nobility.

She may cease to awaken his admiration by her grace and sprightliness, but she can always reign over his heart as a very queen. He may grow careworn and bent, but he is to her a king among men, and always will be.

George Wolf Shinn (1839-1910)

Let there be spaces in your togetherness

Let there be spaces in your togetherness,
And let the winds of the heavens dance between you.
Love one another but make not a bond of love: Let it rather be a
moving sea between the shores of your souls.
Fill each other's cup but drink not from one cup.
Give one another of your bread but eat not from the same loaf.
Sing and dance together and be joyous, but let each one of you be
alone,
Even as the strings of a lute are alone though they quiver with the
same music.
Give your hearts, but not into each other's keeping.
For only the hand of Life can contain your hearts.
And stand together, yet not too near together:
For the pillars of the temple stand apart,
And the oak tree and the cypress grow not in each other's shadow.

Kahil Gilbran (1883-1931)

An ideal marriage

When we have an ideal marriage in view, we must provide the best possible for that life. It is not sufficient simply to give yourself in marriage. You must bring something into marriage ; and the more you bring from the richness of your own character, your own mind and your own soul, the more you will receive from such a life.

Therefore, when a man or woman is contemplating marriage, the first thought should be, 'What can I give to that marriage; how much can I bring to that marriage state that is really worthwhile?' And if those questions are considered seriously, and every effort made to bring to the marital state as much as possible of those things in life that are lasting, that are true, that are genuine, that have real worth—the result can only be what we have desired— something very good and very beautiful in return.

Christian Larson (1874-1954)

My love is like a red, red rose

My love is like a red, red rose
My love is like a red, red rose
That's newly sprung in June :
My love is like the melody
That's sweetly played in tune.

As fair art thou, my bonnie lass,
So deep in love am I:
And I will love thee still, my dear,
Till a' the seas gang dry.

Till a' the seas gang dry, my dear,
And the rocks melt wi' the sun :
And I will love thee still, my dear,
While the sands o' life shall run.

And fare thee well, my only love,
And fare thee well a while!
And I will come again, my love,
Thou' it were ten thousand mile.

Robert Burns (1759-1796)

Let them be patient, and considerate, and charitable

It is well then, to remember that marriage is the union of two imperfect and faulty human beings, and that, therefore, neither of the two is to be surprised at the discovery that the other may be capable of giving offence or of creating disappointment.

The problem to be solved in marriage is how two imperfect beings can get along together without the least degree of jarring. One of the first steps towards solving this problem is to look the fact squarely in the face that each one has faults, and that, therefore, perfect happiness is not to be expected...

If a wife is not perfect, neither is her husband perfect. If he has to endure some disappointment and to meet some surprises - so has she...Let them be patient, and considerate, and charitable.

Let not the wife expect that perfection in her husband which she knows is not in herself. Neither let the husband demand that in his wife which is lacking in him. Knowing that each is imperfect, let both try to make stronger the good points, and to avoid pushing the bad traits into prominence.

George Wolf Shinn (1839-1910)

Hand in hand, on the river of Time

Hand in hand, on the river of Time
We go floating down together;
Soft are the blue skies above our heads,
Balmy the spring-time weather.

Brightly the waters reflect the sun
As we glide in dreamy splendour;
Softly the breezes fill our sails,
Murmuring low and tender.

Sweet are the bird songs upon the shores
Enchanting the scene around us;
With noiseless feet steal the moments by,
Since Cupid, the love-god, crowned us.

Oh do you think, in the after years,
With the glory of youth departed,
We then shall stand still hand in hand,
And heart to heart, as we started?

Anon

Love has nothing to fear from truth

In the final summing up, the things really worthwhile are the heart ties. Intellect and its achievements are sterile, except as they minister to Love in its widest aspect of Service. Furthermore, Intellect can never do its best work until liberated from emotional stress, until the heart is at rest.

Love has nothing to fear from Truth, but selfishness has everything to fear. Selfishness and ignorance are the twin deadly enemies of Love, thriving in secrecy and darkness, but disintegrating in the light of Truth.

Carl Ramus (1872-1963)

Perfect understanding between two souls

Love is the union of desire and tenderness, and happiness in marriage comes from a perfect understanding between two souls. And from this it follows that to be happy a man is obliged to bind himself by certain rules of honour and delicacy.

After having enjoyed the privilege of the social laws which consecrate desire, he should obey the secret laws of nature which bring to birth the affections. If his happiness depends on being loved, he himself must love sincerely; nothing can withstand true passion.

But to be passionate is always to desire. Can one always desire one's wife? Yes.

It is as absurd to pretend that it is impossible always to love the same woman as to say that a famous artist needs several violins to play a piece of music and create an enchanting melody.

Love is the poetry of the senses. It holds in its hand the destiny of all that is great in man and of all that appertains to his mind. Either it is sublime, or it does not exist at all. When it does exist, it exists for ever, and grows greater every day.

Honore de Balzac (1799-1850)

The unity of myself with another

Love is in general the consciousness of the unity of myself with another. I am not separate and isolated, but win my self-consciousness only by renouncing my independent existence, and by knowing myself as unity of myself with another and of another with me.

But love is feeling, that is to say, the ethical in the form of the natural. It has no longer a place in the state, where one knows the unity as law, where, too, the content must be rational, and I must know it.

The first element in love is that I will to be no longer an independent self-sufficing person, and that, if I were such a person, I should feel myself lacking and incomplete. The second element is that I gain myself in another person, in whom I am recognised, as he again is in me. Hence love is the most tremendous contradiction, incapable of being solved by the understanding.

Georg Hegel (1770-1831)

Sonnet XVIII

Shall I compare thee to a summer's day?
Thou art more lovely and more temperate:
Rough winds do shake the darling buds of May,
And summer's lease hath all too short a date:
Sometime too hot the eye of heaven shines,
And often is his gold complexion dimm'd,
And every fair from fair sometimes declines,
By chance, or nature's changing course untrimm'd:
But thy eternal summer shall not fade,
Nor lose possession of that fair thou ow'st,
Nor shall death brag thou wander'st in his shade,
When in eternal lines to time thou grow'st,
So long as men can breathe, or eyes can see,
So long lives this, and this gives life to thee.

William Shakespeare (1564-1616)

The true strength and maturity of love

The marriage relation is the very central, common, and orderly one of society. There should be the same common-sense thought about it that we entertain concerning any other relation in life. We should not be moved by essentially different feelings when thinking of it, or discussing it, than we are moved by when we are considering any other relation of life, as when we are discussing concerning parents and children, brothers and sisters, or even business partners.

I say essentially different; of course there is a difference as each relation is peculiar to itself, and that of marriage is the most important and the most interior of all. But not less than the others does it need wisdom, judgment, thought, common sense.

Love is not made pure by being impulsive, it is not made truly greater for being made self assertive and uncompromising in its demands. It is not to be regarded as any more wonderful and grand by being incapable of calm thought, of wise judgment, of consistent self-control...no love is true which loses its head.

And even when it is true, the lover's love should be regarded as only the beginning, the mere child, which shall grow and develop until it attain unto true strength and maturity of love after marriage.

Charles H Mann (1839-1918)

Do I love thee?

DoI love thee? Ask the bee
If she loves the flowery lea,
Where the honeysuckle blows.
And the fragrant clover grows.
As she answers, yes or no,
Darling, take my answer so.

Do I love thee? Ask the bird
When her matin song is heard.
If she loves the sky so fair.
Fleecy cloud and limpid air.
As she answers yes or no,
Darling, take my answer so.

Do I love thee? Ask the flower
If she loves the vernal shower.
Or the kisses of the sun,
Or the dew when day is done.
As she answers, yes or no,
Darling, take my answer so.

Anon

A true marriage

Husband and wife should encourage each other's spirits, and strengthen each other's hearts, in all that is true and noble.

It should be the aim of the wife to do everything she can to uphold her husband in being faithful in the discharge of his professional obligations. She is to give him hope in despondency, and cheer in gloom, and, above all, she is to discourage anything that is not supremely right in whatever he undertakes.

The husband has corresponding duties in relation to the wife, helping her in her efforts to be a true, a noble woman. A true marriage should contemplate supremely this mutually sustaining each other in all that is good and true, and mutually discouraging each other in all that is evil and false.

It is to be a partnership, then, not for selfish ministrations, but for the encouragement of what is unselfish and beautiful in each other.

Charles H Mann (1839-1918)

My true-love hath my heart and I have his (From *Arcadia*)

My true-love hath my heart and I have his,
By just exchange one for the other given:
I hold his dear, and mine he cannot miss;
There was never a better bargain driven.
His heart in me keeps me and him in one;
My heart in him, his thoughts and senses guides:
He loves my heart, for it was once his own;
I cherish his because it bides.
His heart his wound received from my sight;
My heart was wounded with his wounded heart;
For as from me on him his hurt did light,
So still, methought, in me his hurt did smart:
Both equal hurt, in this change sought our bliss,
My true love hath my heart and I have his.

Sir Philip Sidney (1554-1586)

A true marriage is supremely equal

There is a mutuality in a true marriage, a complemental relation between husband and wife, whereby one recognises in the other at once a want to which he can administer, and a supply which he needs. A wife should behold in a husband a strength to which she would cling, and a weakness which she can make strong.

A husband should see in his wife at once a person to whom he would extend a strong arm for her assistance, and also one to whom he can look for a renewal of his courage, for whose service he is suffering. A true marriage is supremely equal.

Charles H Mann (1839-1918)

Love is the only true foundation

Love, the only true foundation for the marriage relationship, is a complex, not a simple thing. It is not mere passion, the desire for self-gratification or, at the best, self-expression.

True love carries with it the sympathy and understanding of the most perfect friendship, reverence for the soul and mind as well as for the body of another.

For love should embrace all that is best in friendship ; and yet it is quite different from friendship because, of this element of passion, passion not barren and fleeting but fruitful and capable of fulfilment.

Gemma Bailey

From Epistle to Davy, a Brother Poet

It's no in titles nor in rank;
It's no in wealth like Lon'on bank,
To purchase peace and rest:
It's no in makin' muckle, mair;
It's no in books, it's no in lear,
To make us truly blest:
If happiness hae not her seat
An' centre in the breast,
We may be wise, or rich, or great,
But never can be blest;
Nae treasures, nor pleasures
Could make us happy lang;
The heart aye's the part aye
That makes us right or wrang.

Robert Burns (1759-1796)

The basis of all true love

The basis of all true love, which should culminate in marriage, is respect—good, honest, simple, and healthful respect.

Respect for the principles by which the loved one is governed; respect for the honesty of effort by which those principles are carried on in life; respect for each other's character in its intelligence and love; respect for the manhood and the womanhood in its growth and in its efforts for the spiritual blessings of life—these should be the foundations upon which may be built that enduring love, which in subsequent married life shall lead its possessors to unselfishness, to purity, to regeneration.

Let this be the thought which governs in society. Let it be understood by all that sterling qualities of character are what should initiate, and afterwards constitute, the basis of love, and true marriages would not be of such rare occurrence on earth.

Charles H Mann (1839-1918)

Gretna Green

Arise, honest blacksmith!
We stop not for you
Thus early to fit
Or to fasten a shoe;

Your bellows to blow
Or your hammer to swing;
But straightway to wed us—
And here is the ring.

Make haste, honest blacksmith!
The morning is here;
The east is a-blush
Like a blossoming brere;

And we would be riding
The same happy pace
That brought us both here
With the dew on our face.

Now take of our gold
For your service well done,
And take what you will,
For our thanks you have won.

How needless the strength
That we see in your hands,
To forge, honest blacksmith,
The strongest of bands!

Ralph H Shaw (1860 - ?)

Gretna Green is Scottish village famous for elopement weddings, traditionally carried out by the blacksmith. It remains one of the world's most popular marriage venues.

Let the heart of each be open to the other

Let no young husband who has a wife possessing common sense, then, be afraid to communicate to her the true circumstances of his situation, no matter how dark. She is part of himself. Their interests are one; their temporal destiny—one; and it is only by a mutual confidence—an unreserved community of thought and feeling—that true tranquillity can be secured in seasons of adversity.

Let the heart of each be open to the other. Let the husband, in the dark hours of his life, unburden himself to his wife, and the wife to the husband.

If the husband is drawn away from the path of rectitude by the wiles of temptation : if he falls into evil company, or is induced by pressing circumstances to do a wrong, let him never withhold a knowledge of it from his wife—never. She is not fit for a wife if she will not bear a portion of his burden by sympathy—if she will not lend every exertion to relieve him of his difficulty and save him in time to come.

And so of the husband with reference to the dark hours of the wife—her troubles and difficulties. They should be poured out, without reserve, into the bosom of her companion. It is only by a mutual confidence and a mutual sympathy that the burdens of domestic life can be mutually borne.

George Washington Quinby (1810-1884)

Man is for woman made, and woman made for man

Man is for woman made,
And woman made for man;
As the spur is for the jade,
As the scabbard for the blade,
As for liquor is the can,

So man's for woman made,
And woman made for man.
As the sceptre to be sway'd,
As to night the serenade,

As for pudding is the pan,
As to cool us is the fan,
So man's for woman made,
And woman made for man.

Peter Antony Motteux (1663-1718)

An urgent requirement of the heart

Love is an actual need,—an urgent requirement of the heart. It is pure, celestial manna, the bright and ever-gushing fountain of waters, even the ambrosia and nectar of Elysium itself.

Without it life is unfinished, hope is without aim, and man miserable: nor does he come to comprehend the end and glory of existence, until he has experienced the fullness and beauty of an entire and soul-satisfying love, which actualises all indefinite cravings and expectations, and imparts a foretaste of the rich and precious fruits of his future destiny.

Frederick Saunders (1807-1902)

Love

And in life's noisiest hour,
There whispers still the ceaseless love of thee,
The heart's self-solace and soliloquy.
You mould my hopes, you fashion me within ;
And to the leading Love-throb in the heart
Thro' all my being, thro' my pulse's beat ;
You lie in all my many thoughts, like light,
Like the fair light of dawn, or summer eve
On rippling stream, or cloud-reflecting lake.
And looking to the heaven, that bends above you,
How oft! I bless the lot that made me love you.

Samuel Taylor Coleridge (1772-1834)

A cheerful, quiet spirit

One of the secrets of making home-life happy, is the rare faculty of looking habitually on the
sunny side of things—of wearing ever a cheerful smile.

This will dissipate the darkness of sorrow, and irradiate the brightness of joy,—will disarm the former of its sting, and impart a zest to the latter that nothing else can supply.

A cheerful, quiet spirit, that finds its truest enjoyment in accepting life as it is,—determined to make the best of it,—is a boon whose value is above rubies.

A spirit that indulges not in scandal, but draws the mantle of charity over all faults and frailties, and notes only the bright features of character:—such a temper of mind sheds a halo of beauty over the face, a halo that even old age cannot destroy.

Frederick Saunders (1807-1902)

What love is

Love is not made of kisses, or of sighs,
Of clinging hands, or of the sorceries
And subtle witchcrafts of alluring eyes.

Love is not made of broken whispers; no !
Nor of the blushing cheek, whose answering glow
Tells that the ear has heard the accents low.

Love is not made of tears, nor yet of smiles.
Of quivering lips, or of enticing wiles:
Love is not tempted ; he himself beguiles.

This is Love's language, but this is not Love.

If we know aught of Love, how shall we dare
To say that this is Love, when well aware
That these are common things, and Love is rare?

As separate streams may, blending, ever roll
In course united, so, of soul to soul,
Love is the best union of the whole.

As molten metals mingle; as a chord
Swells in sweet harmony; when Love is Lord,
Two hearts are one, as letters form a word.

One heart, one mind, one soul, and one desire,
A kindred fancy, and a sister fire
Of thought and passion; these can Love inspire.

This makes a heaven of earth; for this is Love.

Anon

The married man is stronger than the single

The married man is stronger than the single—is stronger in the great battle of life, and does often succeed where the single man fails. The fact is, that, notwithstanding man's boasted strength, he does not manifest his true nobility and power until he blends his strength with the soft gentle nature of woman.

It is said by some that the most effective missile used in battering down the walls of a fort, is a shot pointed with lead; that the effect of the lead is to prevent its glancing or being crushed by its own momentum.

Be this as it may, experience shows that man can succeed better in battering down life's difficulties when his own harsh nature is softened by the life of delicate woman. Though one would think that his rough, impulsive nature is just the thing to crush through the asperities of life, yet without the influence of woman he is often crushed and dispirited by the force of his own efforts.

George W Hudson

I count my times

I count my times by times I meet thee;
These are my yesterdays, my morrows, noons
And nights; these my old moons and my new moons.
Slow fly the hours, or fast the hours do flee,
If thou art far from or art near to me:
If thou art far, the birds' tunes are no tunes;
If thou art near, the wintry days are Junes, —
Darkness is light, and sorrow cannot be.
Thou art my dream come true, and thou my dream,
The air I breathe, the world wherein I dwell ;
My journey's end thou art, and thou the way ;
Thou art what I would be, yet only seem.

Richard Watson Gilder (1844-1909)

I cannot help loving thee

If the apple grows on the apple tree,
And the wild wind blows o'er the wildwood free.
And the deep stream flows to the deeper sea;
And they cannot help growing, and blowing, and flowing,
I cannot help loving thee.

But if wild winds blew no more on the lea.
And no blossoms grew on the healthy tree,
And the river untrue escaped to the sea.
And they all had ceased growing, and blowing, and flowing,
I'd never cease loving thee.

And till that hour in the day or night,
In the field or bower, in the dark or light.
In the fruit or flower, in the bloom or blight.
In my reaping or sowing, my coming and going,
I'll never cease loving thee.

Anon

Now the rite is done

Now the rite is duly done.
Now the word is spoken.
And the spell has made us one
Which may ne'er be broken:

Rest we, dearest, in our home,—
Roam we o'er the heather—
We shall rest and we shall roam.
Shall we not?—together.

From this hour the summer rose
Sweeter breathes to charm us;
From this hour the winter snows
Lighter fall to harm us:

Fair or foul, on land or sea,
Come the wind or weather,
Best or worst, whate'er they be,
We shall share together.

Death, who friend from friend can part,
Brother rend from brother.
Shall but link us, heart and heart,
Closer to each other:

We will call his anger play,
Deem his dart a feather.
When we meet him on our way
Hand in hand together.

Winthrop Mackworth Praed (1802-1839)

My wife

She who sleeps upon my heart
Was the first to win it;
She who dreams upon my breast
Ever reigns within it.

She who kisses oft my lips
Wakes their warmest blessing ;
She who rests within my arms
Feels their closest pressing.

Other days than these shall come,
Days that may be dreary;
Other hours shall greet us yet,
Hours that may be weary;

Still this heart may be thy throne.
Still this breast thy pillow,
Still these lips shall meet thine oft,
As billow meeteth billow.

Sleep, then, on my happy heart,
Since thy love has won it ;
Dream, then, on my loyal breast ;
None but thou hast done it;

And when our age shall change
With its wintry weather
May we in the self-same grave
Sleep and dream together.

Anon

The tenderness of love

In all the conduct of the conjugal state, then, there should be the most marked and unvarying mutual respect, even in little things: there must be no searching after faults, nor examining, with microscopic scrutiny, such as cannot be concealed; no reproachful epithets no rude contempt; no incivility; no cold neglect: there should be courtesy without ceremony; politeness without formality; attention without slavery: it should, in short, be the tenderness of love, supported by esteem, and guided by politeness.

Affection does not forbid, but actually demands, that we should mutually point out our faults; but this should be done in all the meekness of wisdom, united with all the tenderness of love, lest we only increase, the evil we intend to remove, or substitute a greater one in its place.

Justice, as well as wisdom, requires that, in every case, we set the good qualities against the bad ones; and, in most cases, we shall find some redeeming excellences, which, if they do not reconcile us to the failings we deplore, should at least teach us to bear them with patience; and the more we contemplate these better aspects of the character, the brighter will they appear: for it is an indubitable fact, that, while faults diminish, virtues magnify in proportion as they are steadily contemplated.

John Angell James (1785-1859)

Love bade me welcome

Love bade me welcome: yet my soul drew back,
Guilty of dust and sin.
But quick-eye'd Love, observing me grow slack
Form my first entrance in,
Drew nearer to me, sweetly questioning
If I lack'd any thing.
A guest, I answer'd, worthy to be here:
Love said, 'You shall be he.'
I, the unkind, ungrateful? Ah my dear,
I cannot look on thee.
Love took my hand and smiling did reply,
'Who made the eyes but I?'
Truth, Lord, but I have marr'd them: let my shame
Go where it doth deserve.
And know you not, says Love, who bore the blame?
My dear, then I will serve.
You must sit down, says Love, and taste my meat:
So I did sit and eat.

George Herbert (1593-1633)

Love is the spring of every pleasure

Love, in its primitive purity, is a gentle, pleasing theme—the noblest passion of the human breast—the fairest ornament of rational nature.

Love is the electric chain which connects society and the source of social happiness; for without it, the community of the rational universe would dissolve, and mankind turn savages and roam apart, in barbarous solitude.

Love is the softener and polisher of the human mind; it transforms barbarians into men; its pleasures are refined and delicate; and even its pain and anxieties have something in them soothing and pleasing.

Love is the spring of every pleasure, for who could enjoy the possession of that which he does not love, or perform social duties without feeling endearments of those relations to which they belong.

Love is the first principle of man; it shoots up from the very fountain of life; it cleaves to the human constitution by a thousand ligaments, and can never therefore, be exterminated.

Samuel Stone Hall

Sonnet CXVI

Let me not to the marriage of true minds
Admit impediments. Love is not love
Which alters when it alteration finds,
Or bends with the remover to remove:
O no! It is an ever-fixèd mark
That looks on tempests and is never shaken;
It is the star to every wandering bark,
Whose worth's unknown, although his height be taken.
Love's not Time's fool, though rosy lips and cheeks
Within his bending sickle's compass come:
Love alters not with his brief hours and weeks,
But bears it out even to the edge of doom.
If this be error and upon me proved,
I never writ, nor no man ever loved.

William Shakespeare (1564-1616)

To bear and to forebear

Like government, marriage must be a series of compromises; and however warm the love of both parties may be, it will very soon cool unless they learn the golden rule of married life, 'To bear and to forbear.' In matrimony, as in so many other things, a good beginning is half the battle.

In married life sacrifices must be ever going on if we would be happy. It is the power to make another glad which lights up our own face with joy. It is the power to bear another's burden which lifts the load from our own heart. To foster with vigilant, self-denying care the development of another's life is the surest way to bring into our own joyous, stimulating energy.

Bestow nothing, receive nothing; sow nothing, reap nothing; bear no burden of others, be crushed under your own. If many people are miserable though married, it is because they ignore the great law of self-sacrifice that runs through all nature, and expect blessedness from receiving rather than from giving.

Edward John Hardy (1849-1920)

Love's Trinity

Soul, heart, and body, we thus singly name,
Are not in love divisible and distinct,
But each with each inseparably link'd.
One is not honour, and the other shame,
But burn as closely fused as fuel, heat, and flame.

They do not love who give the body and keep
The heart ungiven; nor they who yield the soul,
And guard the body. Love doth give the whole;
Its range being high as heaven, as ocean deep,
Wide as the realms of air or planet's curving sweep

Alfred Austin, Poet Laureate (1835-1913)

Love renders us wise

On both sides marriage brings into play some of the purest and loftiest feelings of which our nature is capable.

The feeling of identity of interest implied in the marriage relation— the mutual confidence which is the natural result—the tender, chivalrous regard of the husband for his wife as one who has given herself to him—the devotion and respect of the wife for the husband as one to whom she has given herself—their mutual love attracted first by the qualities seen or imagined by each in the other, and afterwards strengthened by the consciousness of being that object's best beloved—these feelings exert a purifying, refining, elevating influence, and are more akin to the religious than any other feelings.

Love, like all things here, is education. It renders us wise by expanding the soul and stimulating the mental powers.

Edward John Hardy (1849-1920)

The passionate shepherd to his love

Come live with me and be my love,
And we will all the pleasures prove
That valleys, groves, hills, and fields,
Woods or steepy mountain yields.

And we will sit upon the rocks,
Seeing the shepherds feed their flocks,
By shallow rivers to whose falls
Melodious birds sing madrigals.

And I will make thee beds of roses
And a thousand fragrant posies,
A cap of flowers, and a kirtle
Embroidered all with leaves of myrtle;

A gown made of the finest wool
Which from our pretty lambs we pull;
Fair lined slippers for the cold,
With buckles of the purest gold;

A belt of straw and ivy buds,
With coral clasps and amber studs:
And if these pleasures may thee move,
Come live with me and be my love.

The shepherds' swains shall dance and sing
For thy delight each May morning:
If these delights thy mind may move,
Then live with me and be my love.

Christopher Marlowe (1664-1593)

The heart of woman

The heart of woman, like the diamond, has
Light treasured in it. There a ray serene
Of heaven's own sunshine ever more hath been;
And though each star of hope and joy may pass
Away in darkness from life's stormy sky,
If man but kindly keep that heart, he'll find
Sweet gleams of consolation there enshrined.

Anon

United for life, love and happiness

In matrimony, as in religion, in things essential there should be unity, in things indifferent diversity, in all things charity.

In matrimony, though it is the closest and dearest friendship, shades of character and the various qualities of mind and heart, never approximate to such a degree, as to preclude all possibility of misunderstanding.

But the broad and firm principles upon which all honourable and enduring sympathy is founded, the love of truth, the reverence for right, the abhorrence of all that is base and unworthy, admit of no difference or misunderstanding; and where these exist in the relations of two people united for life, love, and happiness, as perfect as this imperfect existence affords, may be realised.

Edward John Hardy (1849-1920)

Keep, keep the maiden's dowry,

Keep, keep the maiden's dowry,
And give me but my bride;
Not for her wealth, I woo her,
Not for her station's pride:

She is a treasure in herself—
Worth all the world beside.
Is not her mind a palace,
Wherein are riches rare;

Bright thoughts that flash like jewels,
And golden fancies fair,
And glowing dreams of joy and hope,
That make sweet pictures there?

Keep, keep my lady's dowry;
Her hand, her heart I claim.
That little hand is more to me
Than power, rank, or fame;

That heart's pure love is wealth, my lord,
No more your coffers name!
No statue in your proud saloon,
Can match her form of grace;

No gem that lights your casket,
The radiance of her face.
In giving her, you give me all
I covet in earth's space.

Oh! make her mine, your idol child!
To be my prize and pride,
My star in every festival,
My trust should woe betide,
My bower's loveliest blossom,
Mine own, my worshipped bride.

Frances Sargent Osgood (1811-1850)

True love lasts a lifetime

Perfect love also requires that perfect confidence which nothing can establish but those fullest and most diversified tests which married life alone can furnish. Mistaken they who suppose that years naturally weaken love. Animal love they may weaken; but that blending of soul, that love of moral excellence which constitutes love's crowning perfection, and even quintessence, grows slowly, matures gradually, and reaches its zenith only after the fierce fires of youthful passion have given place to the live coals of mature or declining age.

Matrimony is the very garden and paradise of love, and, therefore, every way calculated constitutionally to strengthen and perfect it, and thereby augment its every charm and sweet. Love seeks the happiness of its object as uniformly as water its level and light diffusion. Kindness accompanies love as surely as gravity matter, and always augments it.

While it is due from all to all, even beasts, and doubly between the sexes, yet love augments it and feelings towards each other. Love's eyes, lips, hands and heart are brimful of desire to make each other just as happy as possible; always saying, 'Please let me do this and that for you.' Neither can make self a tenth as happy as each can the other.

Monfort Allen

The die is cast

The die is cast, come weal, come woe
Two lives are joined together,
For better or for worse, the link
Which naught but death can sever.
The die is cast, come grief, come joy.
Come richer, or come poorer,
If love but binds the mystic tie,
Blest is the bridal hour.

Mary Weston Fordham (1844-1905)

To my dear and loving husband

To my dear and loving husband
If ever two were one, then surely we.
If ever man were loved by wife, then thee.
If ever wife was happy in a man,
Compare with me, ye women, if you can.
I prize thy love more than whole mines of gold,
Or all the riches that the East doth hold.
My love is such that rivers cannot quench,
Nor ought but love from thee give recompense.
Thy love is such I can no way repay;
The heavens reward thee manifold, I pray.
Then while we live, in love let's so persever,
That when we live no more, we may live ever.

Anne Bradstreet (1612-1672)

True love

True love is a sacred flame
That burns eternally,
And none can dim its special glow
Or change its destiny.
True love speaks in tender tones
And hears with gentle ear,
True love gives with open heart
And true love conquers fear.
True love makes no harsh demands
It neither rules nor binds,
And true love holds with gentle hands
The hearts that it entwines.

Anon

Until death shall come

Will it seem to some a strange assertion to declare that many a couple find themselves more intensely attached to each other in the latter years of their lives than they did in the beginning ? It is even so. There has come to be a broadening and deepening of the bonds. They have overcome the inequalities of their lot. They have adapted their characters more completely to each other.

They have outgrown their petulance and irritability. They have a profounder respect for each other. They are more in love with each other than when they were married. They fear no separation till death shall part them.

They took the vows for life, and they will keep them until death shall come.

George Wolf Shinn (1839-1910)

A ring presented to Julia

The name of the bride (or bridegroom) or simply 'dearest' may be substituted for 'Julia'.

Julia, I bring
To thee this ring,
Made for thy finger fit;
To show by this
That our love is
(Or should be) like to it.

Close though it be,
The joint is free;
So when Love's yoke is on,
It must not gall,
Or fret at all
With hard oppression.

But it must play
Still either way,
And be, too, such a yoke
As not too wide
To overslide,
Or be so strait to choke.

So we who bear
This beam must rear
Ourselves to such a height
As that the stay
Of either may
Create the burden light.

And as this round
Is nowhere found
To flaw, or else to sever;
So let our love
As endless prove,
And pure as gold for ever.

Robert Herrick (1591-1674)

I love your lips when they're wet with wine

I love your lips when they're wet with wine
And red with a wild desire;
I love your eyes when the lovelight lies
Lit with a passionate fire.
I love your arms when the warm white flesh
Touches mine in a fond embrace;
I love your hair when the strands enmesh
Your kisses against my face.

Not for me the cold, calm kiss
Of a virgin's bloodless love;
Not for me the saint's white bliss,
Nor the heart of a spotless dove.
But give me the love that so freely gives
And laughs at the whole world's blame,
With your body so young and warm in my arms,
It sets my poor heart aflame.

So kiss me sweet with your warm wet mouth,
Still fragrant with ruby wine,
And say with a fervour born of the South
That your body and soul are mine.
Clasp me close in your warm young arms,
While the pale stars shine above,
And we'll live our whole young lives away
In the joys of a living love.

Ella Wheeler Wilcox (1850-1919)

I loved you first

I loved you first: but afterwards your love
Outsoaring mine, sang such a loftier song
As drowned the friendly cooings of my dove.
Which owes the other most? my love was long,
And yours one moment seemed to wax more strong;
I loved and guessed at you, you construed me
And loved me for what might or might not be –
Nay, weights and measures do us both a wrong.
For verily love knows not 'mine' or 'thine;'
With separate 'I' and 'thou' free love has done,
For one is both and both are one in love:
Rich love knows nought of 'thine that is not mine;'
Both have the strength and both the length thereof,
Both of us, of the love which makes us one.

Christina Rossetti (1830-1894)

I am here to give you happiness

In the realization of happiness we must not forget the ancient statement that 'we must first give happiness before we can receive happiness'; and it is self-evident that the more thoroughly concerned we are with the desire to give happiness to others, the more happiness we shall receive in return.

In married life the principle that each individual should adopt is this: 'I am here to give you happiness, and will do everything I can that may prove conducive to your happiness; and in addition I will do nothing that may in any way decrease your happiness.'

We know that if this were made a positive rule, there would be a wonderful difference; and we all can live up to that rule if our desire to do so be genuine, whole-hearted and continuous.

Christian Larson (1874-1954)

Love is best

I have known a thousand pleasures, –
Love is best –
Ocean's songs and forest treasures,
Work and rest,
Jewelled joys of dear existence,
Triumph over Fate's resistance,
But to prove, through Time's wide distance,
Love is best.

Sophia Hensley (1866-1946)

Other books from Montpelier Publishing
available through Amazon

Wedding Jokes: Hilarious Marriage Gags for your Best Man's Speech
Whether you're making a speech for a wedding or an anniversary, or just want a good laugh, this laugh-a-minute book will keep you chortling at the ups and downs of weddings and married life.

After Dinner Laughs: Jokes and Funny Stories for Speechmakers
This book is packed with clean quick-fire jokes and longer funny stories about all the usual suspects: bankers, lawyers, doctors, estate agents, Scotsmen, Irishmen, vicars, builders, mothers-in-law and many more.

Marriage Advice: Dos and Don'ts for Husbands and Wives
This anthology of advice on marriage contains extracts by well known writers from the past including Jane Austen, Honore de Balzac, Jonathan Swift and Samuel Taylor Coleridge, as well as many lesser known but equally perceptive authors; as relevant today as ever.

The Simple Living Companion: Inspiration for a Happier and Less Stressful Life
This anthology of quotations and passages on simple living from history's great writers and poets will provide inspiration and motivation on your journey to a simpler, happier life.

Non Religious Funeral Readings: Philosophy and Poetry for Secular Services
This book contains funeral readings from some of the greatest philosophers and writers in history. They retain the traditional language of the King James Bible and the Book of Common Prayer, but without religious references, making them suitable for secular funerals.

Printed in Great Britain
by Amazon.co.uk, Ltd.,
Marston Gate.